ANIMAL LIFE STORIES
THE DUCK

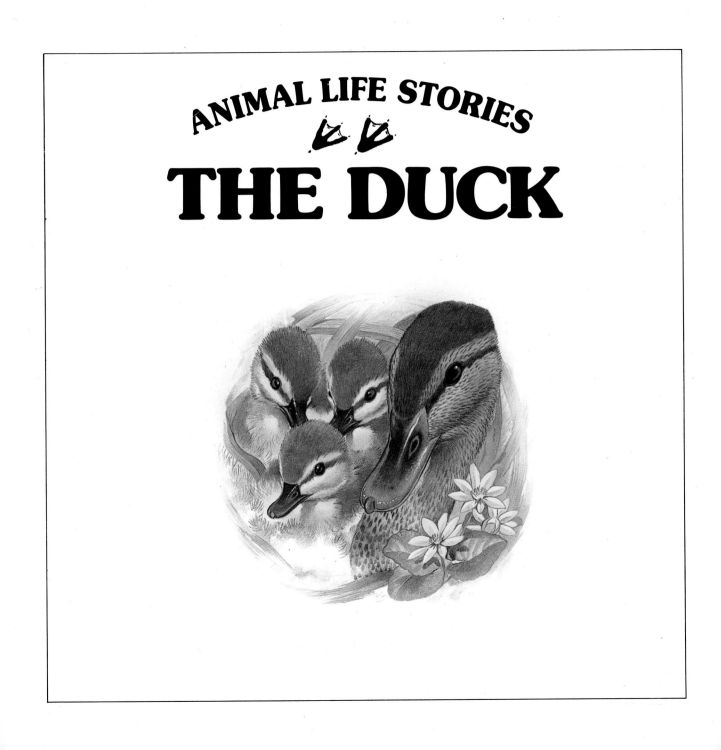

Published in 1988 by Warwick Press,
387 Park Avenue South, New York, N.Y. 10016.
First published in this edition by
Kingfisher Books, 1988. Some of the illustrations
in this book are taken from the First Look
at Nature series.

6 5 4 3 2 1

Printed in Spain

Library of Congress Catalog Card No. 87-51622
ISBN 0-531-19039-0

ANIMAL LIFE STORIES
THE DUCK

By Angela Royston
Illustrated by Maurice Pledger
and Bernard Robinson

Warwick Press
New York/London/Toronto/Sydney
1988

The duck is sleeping with her head tucked under her feathers. Nearby, some drakes are dabbling for food. They stab the water with their beaks or upend to catch tiny water creatures under the surface.

When she wakes up the duck preens her feathers and waddles down to the water. As she swims the drakes circle around and show off their feathers. Each one wants the duck to notice him.

Although she seems not to look at them, the duck has seen them all. As she swims away, she turns her head and nods to the drake she has chosen. He fluffs up his feathers and paddles after her.

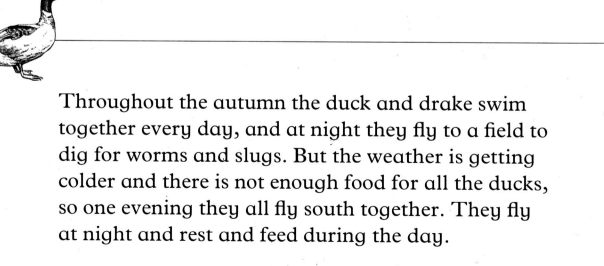

Throughout the autumn the duck and drake swim
together every day, and at night they fly to a field to
dig for worms and slugs. But the weather is getting
colder and there is not enough food for all the ducks,
so one evening they all fly south together. They fly
at night and rest and feed during the day.

The ducks travel for several days, flying over many lands and over the sea. At last they reach a large peaceful lake. Swans, geese, and other ducks are here already, but there is room for all of them.

When winter comes, the edge of the lake is covered with ice. There are plenty of berries and nuts to eat, but the ducks must huddle together to keep warm.

They watch out for danger, too. At night a fox prowls by the lake and an otter hunts across the ice. Both are enemies of the ducks.

When spring comes, the birds fly back to the lake they left last autumn. The duck will soon be ready to mate with the drake. He shows off his feathers to her and chases away other drakes who want her too.

When they have mated the duck looks for a place to build her nest. She finds a clump of grass inside a gorse hedge. She makes a hollow in it and lines it with leaves, grass, and her own downy feathers.

Four weeks after mating the nest is ready. The duck climbs on to it and every day for ten days she lays an egg. Then she settles her warm body over the eggs and waits for them to hatch.

She only leaves her nest to feed in the early morning or at dusk. Before she leaves it, she hides her eggs with a layer of leaves, which also keep them warm.

The duck has no time for the drake now and he goes off to find another duck. For a month she sits alone on her eggs. Then one afternoon she hears a tapping sound. One by one the eggs crack open and out of each egg struggles a wet and bony, chirping duckling.

Gently the duck pushes each duckling out of the nest. As she waddles away to the water they have to struggle to follow her on their big flat feet.

Every day the ducklings swim with their mother and catch insects, but danger is always near. One day a large pike pounces on the smallest duckling, and next evening a marsh harrier snatches another away from its quacking mother. But as summer passes the ducks grow bigger and stronger and learn to fly.

By late summer the ducklings have fine new adult feathers and can fly out of reach of their enemies.

The young ducks no longer need their mother to look after them. When autumn comes she finds a new mate and some of her young ducks find mates for themselves, too. Soon they will all fly south again to pass the winter in warmer lands.

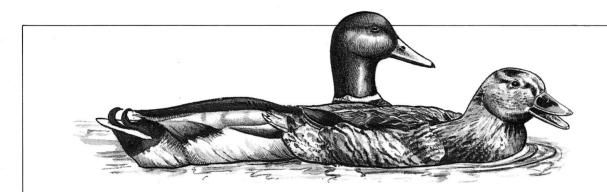

More about Ducks

The ducks in this story are mallard ducks. They form pairs in the autumn but do not mate until spring. When a female duck is looking for a mate she swims with her neck stretched out. The drakes then paddle around her in a kind of dance.

Drakes

Female duck

In winter ducks fly south to warmer lands. They may fly thousands of miles. Some ducks stay and mate in the warmth, but most return north in spring to mate, nest, and look after their chicks. From autumn to late spring the drakes' feathers are brightly colored. But in summer they lose their bright feathers and are the same dull brown as the females.

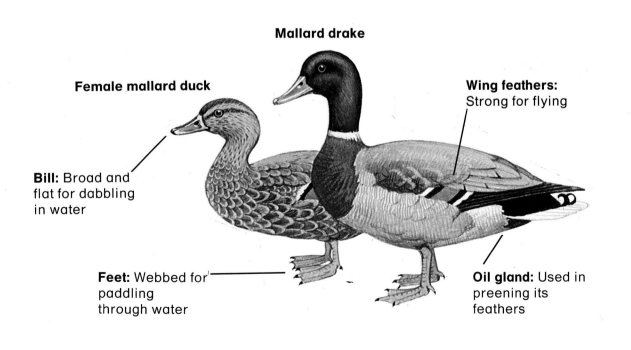

Mallard drake

Female mallard duck

Wing feathers: Strong for flying

Bill: Broad and flat for dabbling in water

Feet: Webbed for paddling through water

Oil gland: Used in preening its feathers

Some Special Words

Dabble When a duck dabbles it dips its head under water and sucks the muddy water through its bill, sifting out insects, fish eggs, and other tiny creatures which it swallows.

Drake A male duck. For most of the year drakes have brightly colored feathers and curly tails.

Duckling A baby duck. Mallards often lay 10 or 12 eggs.

Migrate Ducks migrate when they fly south to spend the winter in warmer countries.

Preen A duck preens its feathers to smooth and clean them and to keep them oily. It presses its bill against the oil gland in its tail and oils each feather.

Upend Dabbling ducks upend their tails to dip their heads deep into the water to look for food.